THIS BOOK BELONGS TO

THE FRIEND OF
THE SAINTS.

My SAINTLY FRIENDS

A CREATIVE ORTHODOX COLORING BOOK FOR KIDS

ISBN 978-0-9959930-4-4 (paperback)

www.creativeorthodox.com

Creative Orthodox

KIDS

DEAR PARENTS,

IN ADDITION TO BEING FUN, THIS COLORING BOOK CAN BE A WAY TO LEARN ABOUT THE SAINTS AND LEARN HOW TO ASK FOR THEIR HELP.

HERE'S HOW TO MAKE THE MOST OF THIS BOOK:

1. SCAN AND LEARN.

SCAN THIS CODE WITH YOUR SMARTPHONE'S CAMERA. CLICK THE LINK THAT POPS UP. SHARE THE COLORED PHOTO AND THE SAINT'S STORY WITH YOUR CHILDREN.

2. COLOR AND PRAY.

I RECOMMEND CRAYONS OR COLORED PENCILS. ENCOURAGE YOUR CHILDREN TO PRAY WHILE COLORING - LIKE ICONOGRAPHERS! THEY CAN ASK THE SAINT FOR HELP OR THANK THEM FOR SHOWING THEM HOW TO BE MORE LIKE CHRIST.

3. CUT AND FRAME.

CUT ALONG THE BLACK RECTANGLE ON EACH PAGE. FOSTER YOUR CHILDREN'S CREATIVITY BY FRAMING THE CUTOUT AND HANGING IT UP IN THEIR ROOM. TRY AN 8X10 FRAME.

THAT'S IT. LET'S HAVE FUN!

CHRIST LOVES US ALL.

HE IS OUR EXAMPLE.

THAT'S WHY THE SAINTS TRY TO BE MORE LIKE HIM.

SAINT MARY ASKS GOD TO HELP US.

SAINT ANTONY OBEYS THE ANGEL AND WORKS
ON MAKING A BASKET.

SAINT ARSENIUS SITS IN SILENCE.

SAINT ATHANASIUS DEFENDS THE FAITH.

SAINT BASIL WRITES THE LITURGY.

SAINTS COSMAS AND DAMIAN HELP THE SICK.

SAINT EPHREM WRITES HYMNS.

ABBA EVAGRIUS WRITES ABOUT PRAYER.

SAINT GEORGE FIGHTS EVIL.

SAINT ISAAC PRAYS FOR EVERYONE.

SAINT JOHN CHRYSOSTOM TEACHES AT CHURCH.

SAINT JOHN THE SHORT OBEYS HIS TEACHER.

SAINT JOSEPH TAKES CARE OF BABY JESUS.

SAINT KYRILLOS PRAYS EVERY DAY.

SAINT LUKE CREATES AN ICON.

SAINT MARINA OBEYS GOD.

SAINT MARY OF EGYPT LEARNS FROM
HER MISTAKES.

SAINT MAURICE LEADS HIS SOLDIERS.

SAINT MENAS STANDS UP FOR HIS FAITH.

SAINT MORWENNA BUILDS A CHURCH.

SAINT MOSES ASKS FOR FORGIVENESS.

SAINT NOFER SPENDS TIME WITH GOD.

SAINT PACHOM TRAINS YOUNGER MONKS.

SAINT PETER THE MARTYR GIVES
HIS LIFE FOR OTHERS.

SAINT PHILOPATER SHARES THAT
HE'S CHRISTIAN.

SAINT PISHOY PRAYS ALL NIGHT.

SAINT POEMEN GUIDES OTHER MONKS.

SAINT SARAH TEACHES THE FAITH.

SAINT SERAPHIM CARES FOR ANIMALS.

SAINT SOPHIA PRAYS FOR HER DAUGHTERS: FAITH, HOPE AND LOVE.

SAINT STEPHEN THE DEACON PRAYS FOR THOSE WHO HURT HIM.

SAINT TEKLA ASKS FOR ARCHANGEL MICHAEL'S HELP.

SAINT THEODORA TEACHES THE FAITH.

SAINT VERENA CARES FOR THE SICK.

MORE FROM
CREATIVE ORTHODOX

Hi!

FINDING VIRTUE,
FUN AND INSPIRATION IN
ANCIENT CHRISTIANITY.

MY SAINTLY ALPHABET: A CREATIVE ORTHODOX COLORING BOOK FOR KIDS
FOR TODDLERS AND YOUNG CHILDREN
A COLORING BOOK WITH 26 A-Z ILLUSTRATIONS OF ORTHODOX SAINTS TO ENCOURAGE YOUR YOUNG ARTIST TO CONNECT WITH THE SAINTS, LEARN THE ALPHABET, AND KEEP FOCUS DURING LITURGY.

POPE KYRILLOS LOVES TO PRAY
FOR TODDLERS AND YOUNG CHILDREN
A FULL-COLOR 18-PAGE BOOK THAT INTRODUCES CHILDREN TO SAINT KYRILLOS. THE BOOK EMPHASIZES HIS LIFE OF PRAYER WHILE SHOWCASING IMPORTANT IMAGERY OF CHURCH, ICONS AND PRIESTHOOD.

"ANASTASIS: THE HARROWING OF HADES"
FOR YOUNG ADULTS & ADULTS
A FULL-COLOR GRAPHIC NOVEL THAT EXPLORES WHAT HAPPENED TO THE OLD TESTAMENT SOULS IN HADES, THE EMOTIONAL BUILD-UP TO CRUCIFIXION AND THE CONSEQUENCES OF CHRIST'S ENIGMATIC DESCENT INTO HELL.

A FOREST IN THE DESERT: THE LIFE OF SAINT JOHN THE SHORT
FOR YOUNG ADULTS & ADULTS
"A FOREST IN THE DESERT" IS A GRAPHIC NOVEL THAT TELLS THE STORY OF JOHN THE SHORT, A HUMBLE DISCIPLE TURNED MONASTIC FATHER. "A FOREST IN THE DESERT" BRINGS THE WORLD OF EARLY CHRISTIAN FATHERS TO LIFE IN EXPRESSIVE PEN AND INK.

FOR MORE CHRISTIAN BOOKS, ILLUSTRATIONS & SAINT STORIES,
VISIT WWW.CREATIVEORTHODOX.COM
USE THE CODE "Creative10" FOR 10% OFF!

Made in the USA
Las Vegas, NV
15 October 2023

79171907R00044